EXPERT PROFILES
VOLUME 8

Conversations with Influencers & Innovators

EXPERT PROFILES
VOLUME 8

Conversations with Influencers & Innovators

Featuring

Jason Bartels

Dr. Sabrina Caliendo

Philip Craik

Jennifer Harshman

Kris Kiler

Teah-Jay Cartwright

Royalties from the Retail Sales of "Expert Profiles" are donated to Global Autism Project

AUTISM KNOWS NO BORDERS;
FORTUNATELY NEITHER DO WE.®

Global Autism Project 501(c)3, is a nonprofit organization which provides training to local individuals in evidence-based practices for individuals with autism.

Global Autism Project believes that every child has the ability to learn and their potential should not be limited by geographical bounds.

The Global Autism Project seeks to eliminate the disparity in service provision seen around the world by providing high-quality training to individuals providing services in their local community. This training is made sustainable through regular training trips and contiguous remote training.

You can learn more about Global Autism Project by visiting GlobalAutismProject.org.

Table of Contents

Jason Bartels – Effective Marketing Funnels for Client Acquisition and Revenue Growth..................................... 1

Dr. Sabrina Caliendo – How Network Spinal (N.S.) Allows You to Live Your Most Optimized Life.............. 17

Philip Craik – UK Craft Specialist 33

Jennifer Harshman – Editing with Empathy 43

Kris Kiler – Reputation Management for Medical Practices 59

Teah-Jay Cartwright – Service, Value and Getting The Most from Your DJ Entertainment........................ 73

Effective Marketing Funnels for Client Acquisition and Revenue Growth

Jason Bartels is the founder and CEO of FunnelMentor. After spending the past decade in the digital marketing space, Jason discovered what it takes for coaches and consultants to get a consistent flow of high-quality clients.

He knows that if you're a coach or consultant earning six-figures a year, you want to become an industry leader that is making seven figures plus. But to do that, you need a proven marketing system that consistently turns prospects into high-revenue clients. The problem is there are so many distractions by "marketing gurus" that are only promoting a part of their marketing plan, which leaves you confused about which method to use and makes you feel frustrated and overwhelmed. Now the good news is, it doesn't have to be this way.

Jason believes good coaches and consultants, like you, deserve an effective marketing system specifically designed for client acquisition and revenue growth. He understands how frustrating it can be to waste time talking with unqualified leads, and spending money on marketing that doesn't work, which is why he specializes in helping coaches and consultants build clear, compelling marketing funnels that predictably convert cold prospects into new clients, and positions them to be able to scale their business.

In the following conversation, you'll get some tips on how to stop wasting time and money on marketing strategies that don't work and instead, consistently acquire high-quality clients and increase your revenue.

Conversation with Jason Bartels

Jason, I have a feeling that there are some people who might be thinking "What is a funnel and why do I need a mentor?" So, give us a little background on your journey of creating your agency, and then let's talk about FunnelMentor.

Jason Bartels: Yeah so, funny enough, my original background had nothing to do with sales and marketing. I started back in my late teens in the concrete and masonry industry and went on to start my own concrete company when I was 25. So, I guess I was in marketing then, but it was old school, using the yellow pages, networking, and meeting potential customers in person. But anyway, I had that company until the middle of 2007 when I got to experience the economy crash and went bankrupt, went through a divorce, and lost everything I built up the previous seven years. As horrible as this was at the time, it was also a blessing in disguise. It left me having this desire to help others succeed in their business, so they won't have to experience what I did.

Through a series of events, I ended up getting into the internet marketing world. So that's kind of where I dove down into that rabbit hole, and once you go in there, it's hard to come out. I always got super excited about getting everything set up; the website pages (we call them funnels now), and all the technical and automation stuff to have a thriving business, and then I would lose interest in continuing with it. I was like, maybe that's not the company that I'm passionate about building... so I'd start another one.

Eventually, after launching several companies, I had this epiphany that since I love and thrive at setting up Automated Marketing Systems, I should focus my time helping others create systems like this as well. And that's what brought me to founding FunnelMentor; so, I can help people build out their sales and marketing funnels and help grow their companies. It's a win-win. I get to do what I love and help others succeed at the same time.

You mentioned going down the "rabbit hole." Is there an opportunity to learn some lessons during that process?

Jason Bartels: Absolutely! And I'm the type of person that dives deep into everything I'm doing. I've taken so many marketing courses and certifications that it would have been a costly college degree. But through learning and implementing, I've discovered what works and doesn't work. Sometimes you learn the best from your failures.

For example, as I progressed through my marketing journey and was in the early stages of building sales funnels, I learned a huge lesson from one of my launches that didn't go so well. I had followed a particular "marketing guru's" method and had invested a lot of time and money to build out this sales funnel. I did everything he said, the exact marking budget (which was quite high), the same type of ads, the same type of funnel; everything was the same. But I launched, and it failed. Then I realized everything wasn't the same, he had a massive following where I did not, and that's one of the reasons I failed. And it's funny, shortly after that he started teaching a different method. It's great to learn certain aspects from these "marketing gurus," but remember, you don't always get all of the pieces of the puzzle, and it's not comparing apples to apples. So, it's from lessons like that, which led me to create a marketing system that works great to acquire high-revenue clients.

How is the marketing system you created different from other techniques promoted by these so-called "marketing gurus?"

Jason Bartels: Absolutely, so I created a system I call the Client Acquisition M.A.P.™ (Marketing Action Plan) which is designed explicitly for client acquisition and revenue growth. It's a step-by-step process that helps coaches and consultants to build a clear, compelling marketing funnel that predictably converts cold prospects into new clients, and positions them to be able to scale their business.

One reason it's different from other programs out there is that it's a very systematic approach where each framework we complete builds upon the other. Plus, it's the exact system that I take my private clients through, as well as the "Elite Consulting" group coaching program that we'll be launching soon. But I would say the main reason it's so different is that my team and I are there to help our clients through every step of the process, it's not just some do-it-yourself course that most gurus are selling. Clients get help from us directly through several different avenues depending on which program they are in.

What do you recommend someone must do to start bringing in their best and highest value target client or prospect?

Jason Bartels: Well, I recommend they get ultra-clear on the number one problem they solve for their clients. Every client I'm working with, I bring back to the first phase (of three) of my Client Acquisition M.A.P.™ that I call the "Clarify" phase.

In this "Clarify" phase, there are three steps, and the first is to get clear on your perfect client and target market. You'll determine the number one problem (Core Goal) that you solve for your potential prospects. Finding this Core Goal that you're going to solve is so essential because it's what you'll use in all your messaging and everything else moving forward.

Next, you move on to step two of the "Clarify" phase which is to "Clarify Your Message." Your message is the foundation for everything you create, for your sales funnel, all your ads, and even talking to prospects on the phone, it all goes together. Then the third step is to get clear on your "Offer" so that it matches your messaging and is compelling enough for prospects to take the next action.

You'd be surprised how many companies create a website, and it's a big clutter that just promotes themselves. So, when you change it around, and you get clear on what you solve, then you can make your message about your prospect instead of about you. It makes your target audience understand what you do because you clearly stated it.

You mention a website that's cluttered... can you contrast and compare a good website to a good funnel? Why does someone need a funnel as opposed to just a website? what's the difference?

Jason Bartels: A funnel is more focused, with one call-to-action. It's like a series of pages that are directing the flow of what a prospect will go through. But with a website, you're going to have all these different tabs on it, for example, you might have an "About me" page, a "Services" page, a "Contact" page, etc. It just gives people too many options and usually causes people to get confused and leave.

Don't get me wrong, I still believe you should have a home base, but make it very clear and concise. I like to refer to my website as the "Home Page Funnel." It has a particular layout that has one call-to-action, to book a strategy session with me, a discovery call.

With a funnel, it just keeps it more focused, more on the point of your primary call-to-action. So, you would create a marketing funnel for each product or service you're offering. In my clients' and my case, I have a funnel called the "Client Acquisition Funnel" that is designed to get qualified prospects to book a call to talk.

Once you have a funnel and get it dialed in, your client flow can become predictable. Let's say you're running ads, you understand that you can spend X amount on ads, and you'll get X amount of leads, out of those leads you'll get X amount that book a call, and out of those calls you're going to get X amount that become clients. So, it just becomes a numbers game, and you can scale it up to increase the number of clients you want at any time.

When you have your message, and your website really polished up and clarified, it feels like your message will resonate much better; and the customer journey of even just getting to the Discovery call improves?

Jason Bartels: That's exactly right. Even starting with the headline, flat out saying what you do. For one, to know they're at the right place, and they're like "Oh yeah this is exactly what I'm looking for." The second thing is having your primary call-to-action button below your headline as well as at the top right-hand corner, so potential prospects know what to do. Having clarity on your pages makes all the difference!

It's almost like you're doing a disservice to your prospects if you're not clear. Because you may have the perfect solution to solve their problem, but if you aren't clear enough to get them to book a call, then you just ruined their chance of succeeding.

You can look at this as having a giver mindset. You have the solution, so make sure they can get it as easy as possible. I believe you've got to give value before you're expecting to get something in return, and I think that's true in anything in life but especially when you're trying to earn someone's business! Especially for those, like my clients and I, that are dealing with higher ticket clients.

So, when someone understands the importance of making their message clear, and this funnel concept makes sense, what else might they get hung up on when considering working with you?

Jason Bartels: A lot of people get hung up on spending money on paid advertising because they look at it as an expense. They sometimes believe "free" methods like posting on social media or creating content is the way to go, which isn't really free, unless you give the greatest commodity of life, "time," no value at all. There's a time and place for that, but it's not when your company is earning low six figures, and you're trying to scale.

You need to look at paid advertising as an investment. It's just like if I told you, "Hey give me a thousand dollars and then in a month I'll give you five thousand dollars back." Would you take me up on that investment? Of course, you'll to do that! So, it's the same thing with doing paid advertising, I think a lot of people get stuck there, but once you get your funnel dialed in, it becomes a numbers game.

For example, let's say your average client value is $10,000. So, you invest a $1,000 in ads to send traffic to the front of your funnel which would be your lead magnet page. Out of that, you're going to get 30 - 40% that opt-in for an eBook, training video, or whatever it is. For simplicity, let's say the average cost per lead is $10. So, that would be 100 leads you get out of that $1000. Now you have 100 leads, and typically if the rest of your funnel is structured correctly, you're going to get around 5% of those leads that will book a call with you. You have five people you'll be getting on a call with, and let's say you only enroll 20% (I like 25-40% better.) That would be one new client. So, you've spent $1,000 on advertising, and if your average client value is $10,000, you just made $9,000.

And let's even take it to the next level and think about two things. Number one is, as you fine-tune your conversation and your meeting with them, maybe it doesn't take you as many calls to bring in that next client. So maybe that same $1,000 might be two clients. Then secondly, consider the lifetime value of the client. So, if you are truly serving and wanting to do the best for your clients, and you bring in the one client and deliver spectacular results for them, there's a high chance that they may give you at least one referral. Now that $1,000 advertising campaign became very valuable!

Also, once people get results, they're always looking for the next thing they can do to advance their business. They're looking to the person that already helped them get results. For example, maybe a client paid ten to fifty thousand to work with me, but they see the value because now they have a client acquisition system set up that took their business to the high six or even seven-figure level. So, they're already happy with the experience, obviously, and then comes the thought of, "Okay, what do we do next?" This is a great place to create new backend higher level products for those clients that are ready for the next level. Maybe it's a mastermind for the elite in that industry that you would charge $50k a year.

So, that one thing that you do may not be the only thing that they need. It might lead to the very next stage in your offerings that helps you take the business to the next level?

Jason Bartels: Yeah and this brings us back to the point earlier about being a giver, and that's just like when you enroll someone in your program or service, delivering on those results. Making sure they get the value you promised or even over-delivering on that is what makes them raving fans! Then they'll naturally progress up your offer ladder.

What kind of clients do you typically work with? Do you tend to find that they are in a specific vertical or niche?

Jason Bartels: The clients I like to work with, are individual coaches and consultants that are making at least 6-figures a year, and their average client value is at least $3000 at the bare minimum. So, they're already established, and they're just trying to get to that next level. Maybe they're at $10,000 a month trying to get $50,000 a month, or perhaps they're at $50,000 trying to get to $100,000.

These clients usually struggle with having the consistency of getting qualified leads. They also might be on the revenue roller coaster where they don't have that predictability of knowing that they'll hit their minimum monthly revenue.

Ultimately, they're just looking to get an effective marketing system that they'll be able to have predictability with their prospect, client, and revenue flow. Plus, they can scale to the next level if they choose. And that's what we do with our clients. I may call it a sales funnel, but really, it's a whole system.

In my system, we take clients through three phases; the first is the "Clarify" phase which I talked about already. The second is the "Convert" phase which is where we're building out the sales and follow up funnels to Attract, Engage and Transform prospects into clients. And the third is the "Capitalize" phase which is where we Advertise, Optimize, and Scale. This third phase is where we really can ramp things up, but that's dependent on the first two phases getting set up correctly. That's why I say it's a complete system, because really everything is dependent on one another, and that's why so many coaches and consultants struggle... they usually only have pieces of the marketing puzzle, not a complete system.

What do you find are some of the common problems that a coach or a consultant should be aware of when it comes to considering a funnel and potentially working with you?

Jason Bartels: One of the most significant problems is "Shiny Object Syndrome." You need to stay focused! When I say FOCUS, I refer to it as an acronym, "Follow One Course Until Successful." We get bombarded with so many distractions, especially in the digital marketing space, because every person out there is promoting the latest marketing fad, and a lot of them have amazing, compelling offers, but usually only a piece of the puzzle.

If you hire someone for their service or join their program, dive in 100%! Do the work they tell you, show up for your meetings or calls, F.O.C.U.S., learn to say no to distractions, and trust the process they have laid out for you. You have to stay committed to the one thing long enough to be successful with it.

How can someone find out more about Jason Bartels, FunnelMentor, and the Client Acquisition M.A.P.?

Jason Bartels: The best way to learn more about me, and to see if my program would be a great fit to help you take your business to the next level, is to go to FunnelMentor.com/Elite. Watch my Client Acquisition MarketingScript™ training video, and then schedule your free Strategy Session to get on a call with me or someone from my team.

About Jason Bartels

Jason Bartels is the founder and CEO of FunnelMentor, a digital marketing company that helps coaches, consultants, and influencers take their companies from six-figures to seven-figures and beyond, without wasting time on unqualified leads or becoming overwhelmed with technology.

He is the creator of the Client Acquisition M.A.P.™ (Marketing Action Plan) which is his signature solution that he takes clients through for creating a clear, compelling sales funnel that turns cold prospects into high-revenue clients.

Jason has started multiple companies over the past 19 years, but his passion always revolved around the system development of the business. He looks at marketing as an entire system, with many moving pieces, and knows that most consultants struggle with getting a consistent flow of quality prospects and clients, which is why he created FunnelMentor. Jason has the privilege of living his passion for helping others create automated marketing funnels that make their companies more effective and profitable.

Contact Jason Bartels:

WEBSITE
FunnelMentor.com

EMAIL
Jason@FunnelMentor.com

OFFICE
(612) 400-7533

LOCATION
Twin Cities Area, MN

FACEBOOK
Facebook.com/FunnelMentor

LINKEDIN
Linkedin.com/in/Jason-Bartels

How Network Spinal (N.S.) Allows You to Live Your Most Optimized Life

"When we transform one life at a time, we are creating a ripple effect to transform many. Each person touches thousands, possibly millions. Even generationally, if you can change a mother or father, and help them be in their most optimal state, then you can change their children's lives, then their grandchildren's lives, and so on. We're creating new patterns even in family relationships, and it changes the paradigm that they will live in."

– Dr. Sabrina Caliendo

Conversation with
Dr. Sabrina Caliendo

Dr. Caliendo, you have worked in two different continents in your 20 years of practice and helped thousands of people. What are the current trends that you are seeing in health?

Dr. Sabrina Caliendo: I've worked in Europe, and I've worked here in the United States. I've been here in the United States, particularly in New York, for the last 13 years. There are so many different trends that go on throughout the culture; the most significant trend that we see now in health is the increase in stress because of our technological age. Life got faster, and there's so much more information that is given to us and that we're receiving and processing every single day, more than ever before. It's unprecedented.

What that has done to the actual individual and, to the culture en masse, is that it has created a lot more stress. We feel that we must be much faster, we must complete our to-do list before we've even made them! That kind of attitude or mindset to life absolutely undermines your health. What we see in our industry, and I think in every single field in health and medicine is that there is so much stress. The latest Research from Harvard Medical School has revealed that all or most diseases are caused by Stress.

Why is that? The reason why is because when we are under stress, especially chronic stress, we engage our Primitive brain and our fight or flight responses. That primitive brain is called the lower brain. It's there to keep us safe, and to protect us from threat. But if we stay in that for long periods of time, and nowadays we've seen that some people have been in that state, or that lower brain state for decades even, what happens is that the brain doesn't regulate the body well.

In fact, all our central organ systems become down-regulated. In other words, sick because we aren't engaging the right parts of our brain. What we want to do is live through our higher brain, which is the upper cortices of the brain, the cerebral cortex which brings us into ease. Wouldn't the world to be a better place if we lived in a state of ease, and grace, surrender, and gratitude? That's a beautifully higher consciousness way to live.

The higher brain controls and coordinates every single cell in your body, every single organ, every single tissue, every single chemical. It's huge. This is a game changer when you can live from your higher brain.

Even the way that you perceive your world changes. When you are driven from your higher brain, the world becomes a much more open, expansive, incredibly abundant, joy-filled place full of possibilities as opposed to an unsafe and scary place, where nothing changes.

The way that we approach our lives changes. If we're in that lower brain stressful state, we're pretty much just trying to get through the day, or the moment and the focus is on ME. It's "How do *I* get through today, and what do *I* need to do in order to get through my task list, how do I escape or avoid discomfort."

Alternatively, if you're living from your higher brain, and you are out of stress it creates a much, much better version of you, so you go from thinking about Me to We, which is huge. It's "how do we all win? What's the bigger picture here?" The higher brain gives you a healthy body, coordinates all your organs, tissues, cells, chemicals and then on top of that it means that you can connect even more deeply to yourself, and more intimately with others. It changes everything. You perceive the world in a much more optimistic way and the world becomes filled with beauty and excitement. You end up following your soul's purpose because you know what it is and feel supported enough in your state to fulfill your "mission."

How would someone recognize or what are a couple of indicators or red flags that someone might be experiencing some stress in their life?

Dr. Sabrina Caliendo: Stress affects us on so many levels; the most significant indicator is, "do you feel that you're living an extraordinary life?" If you don't, then you're probably stressed. It doesn't mean that you must be this entrepreneur that's got a $5 billion company; you must focus on finding the extraordinary. The extraordinary is found in the ordinary if that makes sense. If you're able to go out into nature and admire the beauty in a flower, then you're probably not stressed in that moment. Lack of awareness, not being aware of your surroundings, and not being aware of your behaviors and actions are all Indicators of stress

The next sign of stress is whether you have illnesses?" Do you have any symptoms? That is usually already a red flag that there's stress in your physiology. Another thing would be, "are you someone that reacts, or are you someone that responds?"

Reacting or responding, if you are reacting to situations, and there isn't even a pause to discern, feel through, think through, or to analyze in any way you're probably under stress, and you're probably engaging with that lower brain consistently. If you're someone that's able to respond, and you're able to look at a situation from multiple perspectives you're probably using your higher brain.

Another one of the biggest indicators of stress is how you treat others, and how you treat yourself too. I'm not talking about people-pleasing and treating others well. I'm talking about love. If you feel that you are caring for yourself, loving yourself, living your life from an overflowing cup and that you feel that you're doing that for others and yourself then you're probably doing well.

How do you advise and work with your patients with a holistic approach?

Dr. Sabrina Caliendo: First of all, I don't speak that much to my patients believe it or not, because what I'm looking at are neurological patterns in their system. The work we do is very, very refined and detailed, and we're looking at patterns. When people first come into my office, the first thing that we're going to do is help teach them to reset from chronic stress and access their higher brain so that they can be healthier.

The people that we attract to my office are usually in their 30s to 50s; they're people who want to be their best selves; they want to live up to their ultimate full potential. The first piece of advice I would give anyone is to make sure you are engaging your higher brain.

The next thing is to make sure that you're the one taking charge of your life. What we want to do is empower every single person coming in. That happens, first, with helping them improve their mindset, creating rituals and habits that keep plugging into that higher brain. Plus, making sure that they are living in accordance with their values. We always ask people what their goals are, and then we help them to get there.

I feel like many people think, "A chiropractor comes in, cracks my back, and okay let's see if it helps." Your approach to chiropractic is unique with a technique called Network Spinal. How does that work?

Dr. Sabrina Caliendo: Network Spinal is so unique in chiropractic but also compared to any and every other discipline that exists too. First, we are making extremely big shifts in neurology; you must never say, "cracking my back," to a chiropractor. It's completely inaccurate, but it is the old-school cliché that sticks in people's mind. It's such an insult to the principles, and the artistry of chiropractic.

What we're doing with Network Spinal is we're using an extremely gentle and light touch. There aren't any high-speed, aggressive maneuvers.

We would only use the amount of force you would actually be able to put on your eyelid, on your body and your spine.

What that does is it engages different parts of your central nervous system to create different effects. The beauty of this work is that it trains your nervous system to self-regulate, and self-correct dysfunction in the body from the inside out. This is very different to any other form of Chiropractic. In other words, you are healing from the inside out as opposed to having to take a drug, a painkiller, a supplement from the outside-in, or even being fully dependent on the chiropractor.

What we always want to see is empowerment. We want to give people the tools in their central nervous systems to know that their nervous system is going to be taking care of them. It's teaching the nervous system these new strategies, and skillsets that are unique to this work.

It's just incredible because your body will never forget any of those neural strategies that it has learned. It's like riding a bike; it would be tough to forget how to ride a bike unless there was a major stroke or neurological event that happens to you. It's really pretty impossible. We want to allow the body to be in alignment with its innate, natural wisdom.

I genuinely think that we, as the human species will never fully know and understand what this body is capable of. I see miracles every single day. The work that we do in Network Spinal is the most evidence-based, well-researched form of chiropractic that there is.

I've been in practice for 20 years, and it just blows me away every single day, when I read the research papers, and see that physicists, mathematicians and neurologists, have studied this work, and then you get to see it from that scientific place looking at different nerve scans, brainwave scans. What seems to be a tiny little light touch, or a small gentle impulse that we're putting into the nervous system on the outside creates this ENORMOUS neurological change. If you were to come into our practice not knowing anything it would look like magic. People often ask how a light touch can cause a person's spine to undulate or move in the ways that it does with this work. It looks and feels like magic and it's all very much science-based and reproducible.

Is Network Spinal, the light touch, the way to un-train from old habits and re-train your body to self-regulate?

Dr. Sabrina Caliendo: Yes absolutely. You must be very careful with the types of default neurological patterns that you're training into your body. It even follows through to the way that we behave. If you have a negative thought or a negative behavior repeatedly, what you're doing in your central nervous system and your brain, is you're creating a default pattern. For example, if you went skiing and you were at the top of a mountain, ready to lay down your first tracks in fresh powder or snow and you ski down the 1st time. Let's say this represents a negative thought, or negative behavior, or an illness pattern in your physiology. Then you go back up to the top of the mountain for your next run down the slope; you could choose any other part of the mountain to make a fresh track, but instead, you go down the same path because it's easier.

Over and over, and over again, those tracks in the snow gets deeper and deeper, and it becomes your default. It becomes your default illness, your default behavior, and so on, so you want to always create new positive pathways. Or explore the whole mountain if you were skiing instead of going down the same tracks repetitively. In neurology, we call this neuro-plasticity, which is broadening your scope of what is possible. The Central Nervous System has an infinite number of connections that it could make. We will never be done in terms of how refined your nervous system can be, and what the potential is for you as a result of that!

You recently won a Woman of Honor Award in the category of Sciences for Services to the community, tell us about that award.

Dr. Sabrina Caliendo: First of all, it was a big surprise! The award was given to me at a conference that they do annually. It's a huge Holistic Women's conference here called Gaia's Essence Women's Conference. I think they are in their 11th year now. The award was given to me because I want to empower everybody into knowing what their bodies, and what their physiology is capable of. Not just your physical body, but you, the whole of YOU is capable of.

I do a lot of public speaking, and we hold lots of community events where we educate the public. I have a series in my office called our "Nurture U" series. Every month we speak about a different topic, but in a way, that teaches people to make healthier choices. I always share information that isn't generally well-known, but will be groundbreaking and life-changing information.

We also host monthly Dinner Workshops for the community. These are community-service workshops where we host a dinner, and I speak for approximately 30 minutes on "How to get Healthy Naturally from the

Inside Out." Alternatively, sometimes I'll have other topics too. It's literally to educate the public, and there's no commitment needed, there's no price on it. It's complimentary. We have people come for dinner, hang out, be with our lovely tribe that we've developed at Nurture Wellbeing, we love that! We enjoy being with Like Minded people and spreading our message.

We want to inspire passion, strength, knowledge, and leadership in our community. I think that's why I got that award, because of the amount service that we give to others to raise them up.

When we transform one life at a time, we are transforming many. Each person touches thousands, possibly millions. Even generationally, if you can change a mother or a father and help them be in their most optimal state, you can then change their children's lives, and then their grandchildren's lives, and so on. We're creating new patterns even in family relationships, and it changes the paradigm that you're living in.

Dr. Sabrina, how can people reach out, connect, and learn a little bit more about your practice?

Dr. Sabrina Caliendo: Well, there are two ways. One is through our website www.nurturewellbeing.com. The other is through our Facebook site, which is Nurture Wellbeing. We want to help as many people as we can, so we give a complimentary consultation in our office. A consultation is a conversation about what's going on with that individual. From there, we'll see what their needs are, and if we need to do any tests for further investigation. Everyone is welcome!

Contact
Nurture Wellbeing
1239 Route 25A. Suite 3
Stony Brook, New York 11790
(631) 257-5501
NurtureWellBeing.com

About Dr. Sabrina Caliendo

Growing up in the large coastal resort town of Bournemouth, on the South Coast of England, Dr. Sabrina Caliendo's road to Nurture Wellbeing Chiropractic PC has been a long, exciting, and very rewarding one.

After graduating from the Anglo-European College of Chiropractic in England in 2000, she went on to practice at The Center for Positive Health in Telford, U.K., where she was a top associate. After two years there, Caliendo moved to Shirley, Southampton, where she joined the team at St. James Chiropractic.

In 2004, Dr. Caliendo returned to Bournemouth. It was a homecoming of sort, in the best possible way. She returned to the town she grew up in, with an opportunity to help the people in her community that she held near and dear to her heart. Wave of Life Wellness Center was born and Dr. Caliendo owned and operated the Practice for the next three years. It grew from a generic "Chiropractic Practice" to an energized hub for growth, healing and education.

Wave of Life Wellness was Dr. Caliendo's first Network Spinal Practice. She began practicing Network Spinal earlier in 2004, and made a decision to always work with people to express their full potential, and not just chase pain.

Network Spinal Chiropractic uses gentle touches along the spine to cue the brain to make changes throughout the body, dissipating tension and allowing the person to access parts of the Central Nervous System to regulate the body in the most efficient way. This eventually becomes an automatic response and the body learns to self-regulate in profound ways. This work is gentle but extremely powerful. It creates massive shifts both physically and emotionally, and teaches the body to regulate itself from the inside out. This is a very unique approach, as the body actually learns to "self-correct", and the Nervous System becomes even more evolved.

For Dr. Caliendo, it was so fulfilling to be able to give back to her family, friends, and the wonderful coastal resort town that helped shape her. Wave of Life Wellness Center is where she discovered more of herself – her entrepreneurial spirit and her ability to inspire others to want to achieve more life expression. Her love and passion grew exponentially, and she realized that her profession was in fact, her calling and Souls' Purpose. She chose to live her life in service to others.

Dr. Sabrina Caliendo met her husband, a fellow chiropractor, Dr. Anthony Caliendo, at a seminar in Italy in 2005. Sabrina moved to New York to join Anthony, and they were married in 2007. A year later, the couple founded Practice Wellbeing together in Lindenhurst, New York, which is still in existence today.

After giving birth to her daughters, Anjali, in 2010, and Gioia, in 2012, Dr. Caliendo scaled back to working part-time, in order to raise her family and be closer to their home in St. James. It was during this time, a desire grew to create a community of health-minded people and have her children surrounded by such families in their everyday lives. And in 2015, Nurture Wellbeing Chiropractic PC was born.

Located in Stony Brook, New York, Nurture Wellbeing has become an epicenter for people who want to live their best lives and reach their ultimate potential. It is a center for natural healing through the modality of gentle Chiropractic, and serves the community through education and service. Dr. Sabrina is dedicated to educating her Practice Members, and hosts an array of informative monthly workshops in her "Nurture U Series." Nurture Wellbeing Chiropractic makes donations to many different charities and supports local groups, because Dr. Caliendo strongly believes in raising everyone up locally.

Her mission for Nurture Wellbeing has always been to transform lives through education, inspire passion, strength, knowledge and leadership in the community -- Empowering all to embrace a life of Vitality and full expression of health and transformation naturally.

She is licensed and experienced in many forms of Chiropractic, including Cranial Work, Nutrition, Chirodontics, Pediatrics, Emotional Release Work, and Women's Health. She is at Mastery Level in Network Spinal, a member of the New York Chiropractic Council, a member of the European Chiropractic Union, and a member of the International Chiropractic Pediatrics

Association. She is a published writer and acts as a mentor to many chiropractors in the field.

Dr. Sabrina Caliendo received the "Woman of Honor" Award in the category of "Sciences and Contribution to the Community" at the prestigious Gaia's Essence Women's Health Conference in 2018.

UK Craft Specialist

Philip Craik is Managing Director of Popagami specialising in origami and crafts. Craik launched his company Popagami in 2008 in West Sussex, UK, designing and applying character faces to a traditional Japanese 3D origami animal design.

A Forbes article stated that craft supplies are sold at more than 75,000 retail outlets. A staggering 90% of craft sales are still being made in brick and mortar retailers, not online, and apparently the craft industry market size is around $36bn. Craik saw potential in helping those families looking at enjoying crafts with their families and thus created Popagami as a place to share his designs.

The aim of Popagami is to bring joy to children and adults of all ages with easily folded fun characters that popped to life for hours of play. The Popagami designs are available in various ranges including jungle, safari, fairytale, farm and even endangered species. The items are often filled with treats or used as party favours, finger puppets or garland decorations.

Conversation with Philip Craik

The CEO of the Association for Creative Industries said that 41%, the largest percentage of their crafters in the world, are millennials. Millennial parents are getting involved in kids cross because they see that crafting as a way to bond with their children. How do you feel about this?

Philip Craik: The millennials are grooved in the current way of thinking. In a way, it's like we're talking about sustainability. We're talking about plastic recycling and those kind of things. I believe people are a little bit more aware of what's going on and are generally interested in crafts. Yes, it does help for bonding as well to do these things with your children or the whole family. I think there are a lot of courses in things like Etsy and Not On The High Street too. There's a lot of millennial type people involved in craft making and buying online as well.

Crafts, certainly knitting, used to be seen as an activity for older people but younger people are now taking their knitting needles in groups to Starbucks. In essence, it's now being seen as 'cool' and acceptable for younger generation to be involved in. Would you agree?

Philip Craik: Absolutely. There are loads of fads coming out where really you are making little designs of things. This will always come in and out of fashion. I'm excited to see crafts becoming 'cool' and for Popagami become a widespread fad in the future as well.

Can you tell us about your company Popagami and how it came about?

Philip Craik: The idea came to me when I was working in South Korea. I was employed as a preschool teacher and I was looking for activities and things to do with the children that was Origami related. Origami, as we know, is a huge thing in Asia and so I started making three-dimensional rabbit heads, making them into the Pikachu character from Pokemon. The children absolutely loved that day and even months afterwards they would come in and keep asking for more.

From then onwards, we were making these folded paper characters in all different sizes from ones which are bigger than the preschoolers to tiny ones. We would draw on the faces rather than having them printed. Seeing how much joy the children got from this, it got me to thinking there may be something there. So, I was thinking, okay, if something like that was printed, surely that would be something that people would be interested in.

Things just grew from that moment. We've got animal characters you can change the shape of the ears, colour in crazy colours or you can even have them made from your own photographs. There was such a range of possibilities ahead, I saw the potential that it could actually be something that a lot of people could get involved in. I kept exploring my thoughts and ideas, imagining a child being able to do origami with familiar faces or their favourite pictures.

Popagami is entertaining on a surface level but it also has a certain amount of deeper therapeutic value as well. I'm speaking with special needs teachers involved in this to see how we can best help them. It has a huge potential in terms of who could make use of these. It's not just necessarily people that are into crafts.

People of all ages can enjoy Popagami. We have users as young as five right through to University students, families and workplaces. You can often find us in the cupboard of a grandparent for when the little ones come around to play. I'm currently creating a series of cats and dogs so you could eventually have an app where you'd be able to take photographs of your pets and it will make it into one of the Popagami designs.

The dream would be to see Popagami as a fad in schools. These are fun items you could have in your pocket to fold in the playground or inside on a wet day. Children of primary school age are brilliant at following the instructions. The schools I've worked with so far absolutely love the designs and seeing the children enjoy them so much.

You must be rather creative to make all these new things and constantly come up with new designs. Can you tell us how you first got into art and origami?

Philip Craik: From a very early age I was drawing and my dad was teaching me perspective at eight years old. I'm used to painting and doing crafts as a family. We'd all sit around and paint the same scene. I was also really interested in science as well. In a way, I combine the two. I see what I do as paper engineering. So much goes into the process.

Origami is a major art form in Japan. I believe it started around the sixth century when Japanese monks brought paper back from China and started making their own things with it. Paper is around 2,100 years old from the first century BC. Paper was extremely rare back then and it was mostly used for religious ceremonies.

I studied art and chemistry at A-Level in college and then went to University to study Geology and Chemistry. When I graduated, I started working at Brighton University doing three-dimensional design work, which back then was a brand-new thing of the time. I then moved into engineering for several years. I was fortunate to work in Los Angeles, Mexico and other countries. Then I made a decision around the year 2000 to go into education. I had started educating engineers and before that my first job was with preschools in Seoul hosting arts and crafts sessions. While the two are completely different, to me they beautifully combined both science and art for me.

You really enjoy entertaining people and making them smile while you're out in public. What is it about that that brings you so much joy?

Philip Craik: Well I regularly make my Popagami characters on commuter trains and when I'm out in restaurants. The people around me start whispering "What's happening?" and "What's this guy doing?" The more people who gather round you, the more buzz it creates meaning even more intrigued passersby walk over. They look over and smile and then I invite them to have a go and experience the designs. Quite often people join in and make them there and then with me or I give away a sample they can take home.

When I'm demonstrating Popagami in public, it can feel like I'm presenting a live magic show on stage sometimes. I'm so used to it now I can fold them in the air without a flat surface. This means more people can see what I'm doing and enjoy the whole process and not just the 'ta-dar' moment at the end. When I've finished folding, I blow air into the head which inflates the character. It's a real magical moment when that happens as it's completely new and novel for those watching.

Some Popagami characters are finger puppet size so once they're ready you can have conversations with them and have a lot of fun. I love that I'm able to share my designs with people in such an enjoyable way.

There is a lot of talk about making businesses sustainable and environmentally friendly. Being an owner of a paper based business, how important is creating eco-friendly products and sustainability to you?

Philip Craik: I love the entertaining side to Popagami but I focus on and only do things that are good for the environment. Paper is a finite resource in a way because no trees are growing slowly and we use a lot of paper in the world. I always insist that all my designs are made with recycled paper or sustainable stock. I use vegetable dyes as well so that makes it more eco-friendly as well.

My ethos is always how I can best bring my ideas to life in the most environmentally friendly was possible. For me this is just a way of life. I practice what I preach at home, as do my family, as well as doing my best within the company.

There's been so many issues with things being made in sweatshops, unethical products or plastic. It's a huge issue right now and I'm going against that all the time. I'm even talking to magazine companies about all the plastic cover mounts that holds all the free gifts. We're starting to gain interest in Popagami cover mounts which we make bespoke for their magazine. I do everything I can in my business but also to support others with their sustainability challenges.

The sustainability conversation is big in business right now. Everywhere I turn there's meetings, events and information about it and how we as business owners can tackle this. I believe if we all do something small it can make a massive difference overall.

How can people find out more about Philip Craik and what you're doing and how to get involved with what you are doing?

Philip Craik: The easiest way is to go to my website, which is www.popagami.com.

They can also check out our Facebook page at Facebook.com/popagami for fun how-to videos and more details.

About Philip Craik

Philip Craik is Managing Director of Popagami specialising in origami and crafts. Craik launched Popagami in 2008 in West Sussex, UK, designing and applying character faces to a traditional Japanese 3D origami animal design.

The aim of Popagami is to bring joy to children and adults of all ages with easily folded fun characters that popped to life for hours of play. The Popagami designs are available in various ranges including jungle, safari, fairytale, farm and even endangered species. The items are often used as party favours or garland decorations.

Craik appeared on Dragons Den television show in 2012 asking the 'dragons' for investment in the company. Since appearing on the show, Popagami has been featured multiple times in the media and was even named in a gift list as one of the 50 best books for Christmas.

Through successful business ventures Philip's intention is to help charities and organisations that care for and assist children in need, environmental issues and the survival of all living creatures. Craik leads an eco-friendly business whereby all paper and posted craft packs are made with recycled material.

WEBSITE:
Popagami.com

EMAIL:
brian_craiksmith@yahoo.co.uk

LOCATION:
UK

FACEBOOK:
Facebook.com/Popagami

TWITTER:
Twitter.com/TeamPopagami

Editing with Empathy

Jennifer Harshman understands the dreams and the pains of writing. She knows how scary it is to face that blank page, and, when it's done, to hand your work over to someone who is going to edit it. She knows how important it is to find someone you can trust.

Jennifer's purpose is to come alongside you and walk you through the process, whether you're at the very beginning and have never written anything in your life, or whether you've already published books but are struggling with your new one.

While she does help you with the technical aspects of writing and self-publishing, and can even do it for you, her biggest strength is helping you with the emotional aspects. It's a roller-coaster ride, and it's easier when you have someone there who can tell you it's going to be okay. It's common for people to approach Jennifer when they're afraid or when they don't know where to start or what to do next, and by the end of their conversation, they know their direction and are ready to go.

Jennifer's journey through an abusive childhood and chronic illnesses taught her about integrity, honesty, and the value of hard work. These are the qualities you'll find at the core of everything she and her team do at Harshman Services, to your benefit.

Conversation with Jennifer Harshman of Harshman Services

How did you get started in the editing and publishing world?

Jennifer Harshman: Well, when I was in school, my teachers noticed that I was excellent with grammar, punctuation, spelling, all those types of things. Many of them came to me for help. That really drew my attention to the fact that this is a skillset that not everyone has. So, I've just always done it. In 2003, it came about that a friend of mine was working for a museum and wanted to subcontract out the editing work of a two-volume set to me and they needed it put into British style because it was going to be published in London. And I said, "I don't know how to do British style. I know American grammar and such."

She said, "Well, I know that you taught yourself how to catalog books in just a couple of hours, and most people go to school for a master's degree for that. If you can teach yourself to catalog books, you can teach yourself to edit in British style. Go!" And so, I did, and they loved my work and wondered why I was not editing full-time professionally. That was the billboard telling me I should be editing a lot more than I had been.

Is that how most editors break into the industry?

Jennifer Harshman: Sometimes people will major in English or journalism, and then they'll go to work for a newspaper or for a publishing house and do editing in-house for several years before they decide to go freelance. Other people just decide to become editors whether they have any experience or qualifications. The way that I went about it was a little different than normal in that I used my education and work experience in other fields and added to it with self-study to become an editor and coach.

I had done it a little bit more all through college, so I knew that I had the skills, but I did really take that comment as the sign. I had been looking for something that I could do at home with my kids to homeschool them. And I knew that I could not hold down a traditional job because of my health issues. So, it was just the perfect thing. I started contacting friends. I mentioned that I had done those books, and some other people said, "Hey, I've got a book!"

One gentleman said, "My wife wrote a book and published it, and it's full of errors, so she knows she needs to pull it down off Amazon and have it edited now." She self-published on Amazon and started getting some negative reviews because she had not had it professionally edited. She had several of her English teacher friends and others review it, but it had not been professionally done. When she started getting negative reviews, she realized that she really did need to invest in editing. And so, I did that one. Everyone I served was thrilled and told people, and one thing just led to another.

Who do you typically help with your editing services?

Jennifer Harshman: I serve all types—fiction and nonfiction authors, publishing houses, small presses, a wide variety of other businesses, and entrepreneurs. I even edit for other editing agencies. The common denominator is that the writing is helpful.

At what stage in the writing process do you come in to help an author?

Jennifer Harshman: Sometimes people will meet me at the very beginning, and they'll say, "Oh, I've always wanted to write a book!" Eighty-four percent of Americans want to write a book, but only a very small percentage follow through and actually do it. For people who haven't even started yet, I take them by the hand and walk them through the whole process. We'll mind map and brainstorm and, bringing in my extensive reading experience and keyword research (another skill set of mine), figure out exactly what needs to go in their book as well as what might be set aside for another one later on.

Then we go through the writing process, and I shape the book as it goes. When it's written, I edit it and get it ready for publication. We do the formatting and everything that they need including uploading to Amazon and setting up their book page and author page. Some call us a one-stop shop now. It's really grown over the last decade.

Sometimes people will meet me in the middle when they've already started. They know what they want to write about, but they get stuck. They might get all their ideas out, realize that it is still incomplete, and say, "I don't know where to go with it!" So, then they'll meet me, and I'll help them finish fleshing that out, get the rest of it written, get it edited, get it published.

And sometimes people have done very well on their own. They know all the things they want in it. They're done with the outlining, development, and writing. But they know that they need to have it professionally edited, so then they'll come to me at that point. I really do meet people anywhere along that road.

What are the different levels of editing that are available?

Jennifer Harshman: I have a metaphor to explain the different types of editing. Imagine that you're in a commercial airliner flying over the Midwestern United States. You can look out the window and see different colored patches on the ground. You can tell that those things are fields, but you can't tell if that particular patch is a soybean field or a cornfield. Developmental editing comprises the very big-picture items—the things that you might see from 10,000 feet if you were looking at your book. These are things like the topic, what belongs in and what does not, which chapters go where, what needs to be covered and whether it's covered well enough, things like that.

Line editing is where we look at the languaging. And that's being in a crop duster. You're lower to the ground. You can tell it's absolutely a cornfield, but you can't get any details. Is it sweet corn, is it field corn? How many rows, how many acres? Those types of things are not apparent because you're not close enough to it yet. So, with line editing, we'll look at each sentence as a whole. We'll look at the languaging in it. We'll look at each sentence within its paragraph. We'll look at each paragraph within each section. So, it is close to developmental editing, but it's on a much more micro scale. Some consider it to be developmental, some mechanical, and some say it's both. Regardless of where you categorize it, it's an important piece.

And then copy editing is where you're walking on foot through that cornfield. You can count each individual cornstalk and get a much closer look. That's where we look at each individual word. Is it spelled right? Is it used correctly? Is it punctuated properly? All of those activities that are what most people think of as "editing" fall into copy editing. This is what is the most visually apparent to readers and what they mention in reviews when it's done poorly or not at all.

Proofreading is the very micro level where we're going to peel back the husk on an ear of corn and look at every individual kernel. We inspect literally every character in a book during this phase. Proofreading comes after formatting. Many people use the term "proofreading" when they are actually referring to copy editing.

Why are so many levels of editing and review necessary?

Jennifer Harshman: If you only do one type of editing but you need more than one type, then you're going to be missing quite a bit. For example, some people might ask for copy editing and proofreading so that it will look good as far as reading individual sentences or paragraphs, but if you look at the book as a whole, there might be some gaping holes. In that case, developmental editing was needed, too.

An editor is first and foremost a reader. Even though the author or the corporation might be the one who's paying the bill, our client is really the reader. That's who we serve, and we want to serve the reader through the author. Of course, the author benefits as well because their book or other piece of writing is coherent and people can receive their message more easily. But really and truly, the end user is the reader.

Often authors suffer from what we call curse of knowledge, which is where they know their field of expertise so well that they forget what it was they did not know as a beginner. As editors, we try to put ourselves in the shoes of a beginner who is reading the book. Sometimes we ask a lot of questions of the author. We might ask for clarification. We might ask for simplification. In my notes to my clients, I make a lot of comments like, "At this point in this book, your typical reader may ask this specific question. If you want to address this, this would be a good spot." It helps the author get around that curse of knowledge to serve their readers better.

Many first-time authors comment on the emotional rollercoaster that comes with the editing and publishing process. What are your thoughts on that?

Jennifer Harshman: A big part of why I got into editing is because some of my friends are authors. They would go the traditional publishing route and then they would get their book back and say, "It's not even my book anymore. It's been changed so much." And I would tell them as gently as I could that they were correct. It was not their book. They signed a contract, and at that point, ownership transferred to that publisher. The author would just receive some royalties. So, if they want to keep their next book as their own book, then self-publishing is the route they'll want to go. It gives them all the control over what happens.

As an editor, I wanted to be sure that all my clients would feel much better about the process. I've seen people in tears, and that to me is just wrong. When somebody is going through this process, it's difficult, and I get upset when I see other people not treat them with empathy. Just be a human, you know! Just put yourself in their shoes.

When I train my team, the number-one principle is The Golden Rule. If you were to read this comment about your own work, would you feel respected? Would you feel that the person cares and is taking the time and giving you the attention and the support that you need? Or are you going to feel like they just slashed your baby? I compare it to going through surgery. When you have your book edited, it is a difficult process! Even in the best situation, it's not easy. You have put so much of your heart and soul and effort and time into it. It may have been months if you're a quick writer. For most, it may have been years. It's your baby, and you're handing it over to someone to shape it and to change it. And it's frightening and stressful. Even for the toughest people, it's really hard to do. So, I want authors to feel we're walking them through it, holding their hand, we're making it less stressful, less scary—and that we respect them and what they're trying to accomplish. We know how important it is. So, every comment needs to be clear and kind. That's our goal, to help them and their readers, and to do it as gently as possible.

What's it like for you when you see an author with their book?

Jennifer Harshman: When you hold your book in your hands... There's no feeling like it. Most authors will take a picture with their books. They'll order a box of books for an event that they're having or to distribute to their friends and family, and they want to take pictures because it is just such a touching moment, and they are so excited. I don't even know how many authors have emailed or Facebook messaged me a photograph of themselves like, "My book's here, Jennifer!" They're just over-the-top, over-the-moon excited. It's that way for just about everybody.

Do you recommend that your authors focus on printed books or electronic books?

Jennifer Harshman: I think there's a place for both. Of course, we did hear that prediction, all of the "print is dead" headlines. And at the time, I thought, "No, I don't think so." I think there will always be some people who love the feel of a physical book in their hands. Sometimes a print book is more portable than a device. You can take it to the beach, for example. You don't have to worry if sand gets into a paperback book. And there's "screen fatigue" to consider, too. People are using computers and phones and Kindles and looking at screens almost all day, especially if they work in certain industries. They're looking at a screen all day long as part of their job. Then if they want to read, it's going to be difficult because their eyes are exhausted. Print tends to be easier on the eyes, and people are gravitating back toward that. The pendulum did swing toward eBooks for a little bit, and now I think it's going to kind of come to rest. The world is big enough for both print and electronic books.

Is there a particular genre or type of author you especially like working with?

Jennifer Harshman: Some people think of themselves as a writer or someone who needs that creative outlet. They enjoy the process and the result. Then there are people who don't really think of themselves as writers, but they know that they need to have a book or they need to produce content for their blog on a regular basis, and they feel stuck or that it's a really difficult process. Those are the people I really love to help. Sometimes they'll say, "This is the thing that I want to do, and this is where I want to go with it."

They know the purpose for their book, and it's not necessarily to hit the bestseller lists. They're not necessarily looking to retire on their income from the sales of their book, but they're using it as a tool to open more doors. Some will use their book to get speaking engagements. Some will use their book to distribute their message to their foundations or their church members.

There is a variety of purposes, but for the most part, having a book helps to open doors and create opportunities where other things just don't. We even have a phrase in our language to indicate the credibility being an author gives: "She wrote the book on that," which indicates that she is the authority on that topic. It does carry quite a bit of weight to be able to say that you wrote a book, even in an age when just about anyone could write a book.

What are some considerations for authors deciding between self-publishing and traditional publishing?

Jennifer Harshman: About a decade ago, it was still a little iffy as to whether self-publishing was the way to go. There was kind of a stigma to it still, and some people would look down on self-published books, even calling them "vanity published" or say that somebody went to a "vanity press." And there was some reason for that because usually people didn't have professional work done. They usually didn't edit it, and sometimes their printers didn't produce the greatest quality. Many of those presses were and still are downright predatory, too, so authors should be careful. But Amazon has helped a lot with printing issues for self-publishers. They provide good quality with their KDP program. And nowadays, more people are realizing the value of editing. I think self-publishing can be a kind of double-edged sword. On one hand, anyone can be an author, and on the other hand, anyone can be an author. Some of the stuff that you'll see produced is of high quality. Some of it is of very poor quality.

I do see more people going toward self-publishing mostly because they have the control. Another factor is speed. For example, perhaps you want to have a book out this year because you're going to several conferences or you're going on a speaking tour. In that case, self-publishing is the only option because a traditional publisher, if you're picked up by one, is going to take 18 months to two years to release your book. That's their typical cycle. So, if you want to do something that's just around the corner, then you definitely want to do self-publishing. I just see more people doing that.

Traditional publishers need to look out for their bottom line. It's just as it is with any other business, and they need to go with the authors that are going to be marketable. Usually nowadays, if you do not already have a platform, if you are not already significantly well known, they're not going to be interested unless the topic of your book is something that has wide mass-market appeal. Most people who want to write a book really don't fit into that category at all. They have a particular "heart issue," a particular passion, or a specialty, something that relates to a smaller audience. To me, it's not any less viable or any less important just because it's smaller. But to a traditional publisher, it is, because they have to look at their bottom line. That's why self-publishing is so great because it opens up the ability to publish even if an author has a smaller platform or no platform but a good message.

Please note that self-publishing doesn't preclude you from entering traditional publishing later on. There have been some well-known books that were self-published and were later picked up by traditional publishers because they did so well that the books got on the traditional houses' radar. So it doesn't shut the door forever as some believe it does.

Definitely do some research and decide which route you want to take. For most people, it just takes a couple of minutes to evaluate which way they want to go. Then I would say, "Know your purpose." What do you want to accomplish with this book? If you begin with that end in mind, then you can work backward to see which steps you need to take to get there.

You recently announced a new program to help authors self-publish their book. Can you share some details about it?

Jennifer Harshman: I have a 12-week program, which is start to finish. That would be for people who haven't yet started to write their book. They might know the book's topic; they're experts in their field. We walk them through from the very beginning, planning it out all the way through the writing process, through the editing process, and then get it published.

There is also a shorter one, a six-week program. It's for people who have written at least the bulk of their manuscript. We walk them through the editing process and the publishing process in just six weeks. There's more, of course. We have something for everyone who wants to make a difference with their writing. Stay safe, and find an editor with empathy so you can have a bigger impact. Here's to your success!

About Jennifer Harshman

Age three was a big year for Jennifer Harshman. That year, she taught herself to read and write, and she hasn't stopped since. She's read more than 17,700 books, and because she reads more than 10 million words a year, adds to that figure almost daily.

Jennifer bore the label "twice exceptional" along with severe abuse, but has brought good out of it all. Combining these and other factors with such an immense number of books read gives her a unique ability to be the bridge between writers and readers.

She coaches and consults with subject-matter experts, communicators and other leaders, entrepreneurs, authors, and publishers so they can get helpful writing out into the world where it can do more good. Jennifer began editing professionally in 1992, has edited tens of thousands of pages, and now serves as a writing and publishing expert for publishers and independent authors alike.

WEBSITE
EditingWithEmpathy.com

EMAIL
jennifer@editingwithempathy.com

PHONE
(618) 315-4036 (Text message only)

FACEBOOK
Facebook.com/Jennifer.Harshman

TWITTER
@JRHarshman

CALENDLY
Calendly.com/jennifer-harshman/zoom-meeting

Reputation Management for Medical Practices

Kris Kiler is the Founder and President of Net One Click, a marketing agency that makes it easier for small to medium-sized medical practices to engage with current and prospective patients through their Search/Social/Stars methodology.

Since 80% of people start their search for a healthcare provider on Google, it's important for a medical practice to appear at the top of the search results. With the ubiquity of Facebook, Instagram, and other social media platforms across all patient populations, medical practices also need to have a presence on those platforms. Online reputation and star rating sites like Yelp and Healthgrades have become exceedingly important for practices to both attract new patients and retain existing patients.

To help their clients better manager their star ratings and reviews, Net One Click created their Patient Promoter system, a proven, results-driven solution that gives medical practices a simple way to manage their online reputation. Patient Promoter helps practices measure the patient experience, improve practice reputation, and capture patient feedback.

Conversation with Kris Kiler
of Net One Click

How did you get started helping medical practices with their reputation management?

Kris Kiler: Well, I have four children so healthcare is a pretty big issue as is the quality of care of care that they receive. As somebody in marketing, when I take my kids to the doctor, I want them to have a good experience. I've been doing marketing for about 20 years, and about 10 years ago decided to focus on healthcare. In my previous business, we worked with hospital systems on increasing patient experience through personality profiles and understanding the patient from their level of psychology and how to adapt to their unique perspective and focus on the quality of care and customize the care according to their particular personality. So, I had some experience in the industry and I just have a personal passion, a personal interest, in helping medical practices do better and continue to grow.

What is the biggest challenge that medical practices face when it comes to their online reputation?

Kris Kiler: Their biggest challenge is "Help us with Yelp." The docs and practice managers all are really frustrated with the process. Patients can lie on Yelp and Yelp won't take down reviews unless they have a legal order. So, most doctors have a real big problem with Yelp. So, that's the number one thing. Also, "How do we ask patients for reviews? How do we know whether the patient has had a good experience so that we can have a reliable source of someone who can go and leave a five-star review?" In response to our client challenges, we built a system in Patient Promoter that does that, and segments out those patients, so that we can figure out who will leave a review and who won't.

Are there situations when Yelp and other review sites can be helpful for their practices?

Kris Kiler: Doctors recognize the value in having a high five-star review, but most of the doctors don't want that to be the primary indicator of their performance as a physician. Mostly because they don't know how to ask patients for reviews and they're not comfortable with it. So, they think that they have to ask a patient, "Hey, will you go give me a review?" There are a lot of issues around having a community decide whether you're a competent doctor, which a lot of doctors are really frustrated with because most often it's the patients who have had a negative experience who go on these sites and post a review and they can't control for that.

When these physicians go to their practice's profile and they see they have a two-star review, and they feel like they are doing a good job at serving patients, it doesn't feel good. Not saying that any of this is bad, because we all have our ego invested into our profession. It's just that Yelp highlights all of the bad things about what happens at the practice. Just like Rotten Tomatoes can ruin a movie if it has a low rating, it's no different for a medical practice or any other business that's on Yelp.

If you have a two-star rating, the research shows that only 13% of the people will even consider going to your business.

So, is getting a good online reputation simply a matter of getting more five-star reviews?

Kris Kiler: Well, the practice has to deliver quality care, obviously. That's one thing we want to focus on, but as far as asking for reviews, we don't recommend they approach patients. Mostly because that's a conversation you don't want to have when someone is in the medical office. When they have an appointment, depending on what you're talking to them about, it could be something very sensitive and you don't want to be asking them for a review on Yelp when they're leaving the office. That's why we want practices using the Patient Promoter system. They can email them, ask them about how their experience was, and then go from there through the process.

What else does a medical practice need to consider beyond their online reputation?

What we say is there are three critical things that every medical practice needs to focus on in order to get and keep patients. The three things are; search, social, and stars. "Search" would be Google. The research shows that 8 out of 10 people start their search for a healthcare provider on Google, or on a search engine. So, if you're not showing up on Google, whether it's your local business page with your address and your phone number or it's your website—if you're not showing up on the first page, it's not likely patients are even going to consider you as an option.

As far as the "Social" aspect, the data has shown that patients want medical practices to share information on social media. They want to be communicating with them and seeing posts go out on Facebook, Instagram, wherever. So that's another aspect of it. Then the third is "Stars," which kind of crosses all the components. Yelp, Facebook, Google--your star ratings on those three sites are going to be an indicator of how good you are as a practice to the patient. Prospective patients are going to be looking at those star ratings as a method to make their decision to select you as their medical provider.

Can a business still be successful if they ignore their reviews and online reputation?

Kris Kiler: It would be like driving with blindfolds on. You can ignore it all you want, but at some point, you're going to run off the road. The research has shown that your star rating on these sites is shown to be the number one factor for whether a patient chooses you. It also is going to factor in whether somebody continues to go to you. So, if a current patient happens to go on Facebook or Yelp, and they see that you have a one or two-star review, and they see all these people complaining and posting these negative comments--and it doesn't have to be a lot, it could be one every month, depending on your patient volume--12 one-star or two-star reviews in a year can really negatively affect the practice.

Monetarily speaking, research has shown that in terms of new customers, if you have a two-star rating, only 13%

of the people will even consider the practice or the business. When it goes up to three stars, it jumps up to 57%, so about 6 out of 10 people, and then if you have a four-star rating, it goes up to 94%. So, a one-star rating can mean the difference of three to four people out of 10 picking your practice. These sites can have a huge impact on the bottom line of the practice.

Even after they understand the fiscal impact, what keeps medical practices from doing anything about their online reputation?

Kris Kiler: I think it's a level of feeling competent around the tools and strategies associated with marketing the practice. I think with an industry like healthcare, you have doctors who have spent a lot of time investing in their education and their skills as a doctor. So, when they find themselves running a practice and having to decide what marketing vendor to select, or what to do on Facebook, it can feel really overwhelming for them, because they want to be competent about that particular subject matter. So, it's really just a factor of educating them and holding their hand and making sure that they understand what the process is and meeting with them on a consistent basis and updating them and letting them know what we're doing and making them feel at ease with all the things we're doing, to make sure that they know that we understand that we have their reputation in our hand and we take that responsibility seriously.

What are some mistakes you've seen medical practices commit when they start down the path of managing their online reputation and reviews?

Kris Kiler: I would say there are probably three things. The first mistake is not paying attention to the content that they're developing. Too many practices develop their website where they buy a standard website and they think they're done after the pages with the doctors are up and the address page, and they have a page with a view of the services. The thing is that Google rewards websites with unique and ongoing content. So, paying attention to things like building your blog and adding video are really going to help your long-term search engine optimization, which doesn't have an immediate impact, but it's a key factor in being competitive over the long term.

Second, on Facebook/Social side of things, the mistake is really focusing on quantity rather than quality. How many followers do we have? or how many times do we post in a week. If you understand Facebook and know how to use their system, you don't have to post every day and you don't have to have 5000 followers from all over the country to look good. The goal is to focus on your local market and get the followers that actually are real and make sense, and post real and relevant information for those people. You don't have to focus on posting three or four times a day. I see a lot of that happening.

Finally, the last mistake is thinking that if they get a few five-star reviews that they're done. So, practices think that they can spend a couple months generating some reviews, bump up their star rating, and think, "We're done! We got to four stars and we can stop!" But it's a long-term game and you have to think strategically about all three of these things.

Do you have any examples of practices that were able to turn things around using the methods you described?

Kris Kiler: We had a practice about four years ago and we struggled with the exact problem that we talked about earlier, about how to ask patients for positive reviews. Do we reward them? Do we pay them with Starbucks gift cards? That's not really recommended.

So, we built the Patient Promoter system to solve that challenge. We were getting two five-star reviews approximately every nine months. So, without asking people and being proactive, we weren't getting very many five-star reviews. We were getting a consistent flow of one and two-star reviews just based on the volume that we had at the practice.

After we implemented the Patient Promoter product, the following nine months we generated an 1100% increase in five-star reviews. We maintained about the same level of one-star reviews but those five-star reviews helped us overcome that hurdle of figuring out how to ask patients to leave a review and start being proactive in managing the reputation, and ensure that when new patients go to our pages, they see a star rating that is reflective of the quality of care that they're going to be receiving.

Are those results an anomaly, or can other practices expect similar results?

Kris Kiler: Yeah, the average practice that we have has anywhere between 40 and 100 patients a day. So, if you're sending out a survey and you're asking people about their experience every day, and you send the message that you're concerned about the level of quality of care that they're receiving and what their experience is like at the practice, people are going to respond. You can go from getting one five-star review in a month to getting seven or eight, I mean, it's as easy as that. It's a huge jump. Just asking every patient how their experience was and if they're interested in referring you to a friend or family, can have a big impact on your star ratings. All of our customers have a very consistent and solid flow of five-star reviews every month.

There's also a lot of research that shows that people are 10 times more likely to go leave a negative review as opposed to a positive review. So, people who are irked for whatever reason--it could be the parking, it could be because they were late and they're frustrated with their own life issues, it doesn't necessarily have to be about the practice, but if they had a negative experience-- they're more likely to go leave a review than people who are happy. People who are happy don't ever think about it, right? You expect good service, so when you go to a restaurant or any business, you don't expect to have a bad experience. So, when you leave and you've had a great experience, you don't think "Oh, I'm going to go leave a review on Yelp," that's just not the first thing people think about. So, by asking people and reminding them that the best the thing that we can do is have our patients say great things about us--that's how we're going to stay in business and how we're going to grow the business. And we would really appreciate it if you would help us out with that. That works. It's not in your face.

Do medical practices have to offer incentives to get more positive reviews?

Kris Kiler: No, not at all. All of the reviews our clients get are completely organic. So, we ask them how their experience was and they respond. Then we ask them, would you mind going and leaving what you just said about our practice on one of these sites? And that's it. So, they're all honest and unique patient-generated reviews. We don't give them fabricated testimonials to copy and paste, or anything like that. So, yeah, it's a great system.

What's the first thing you would recommend to a medical practice that wants to improve its overall marketing?

Kris Kiler: The first three questions that we ask every medical practice that we work with is to ask yourself who you are as a practice, how are you different from other medical practices, and why should patients pick you. What makes you different from other practices? Why should I pick you over other people? So those three things, if you focus on those three things, that's kind of the core foundation to begin building a really good marketing program.

If a practice is choosing a company to help them with marketing or reputation management, what are some things they should keep in mind?

Kris Kiler: That's a good question. I think the biggest thing is don't be wowed by buzzwords. A lot of companies will use fancy terminology but won't focus on the facts of the service. So, they're not data driven. We feel it's important is show the performance of the marketing program every month. A lot of places won't want to talk about the data, they won't want to talk about the how you're growing your web traffic or how your advertising is performing.

You really want to focus on the data and the methods behind how the business is going to get you the results. Because that's really the most essential thing to any program. And do your research. Some providers have no experience. They have great sales people, but their delivery is poor. So, I would recommend doing your research and trying to get someone who focuses on performance-based marketing as opposed to just posting twenty-five times on Facebook or setting up a simple website.

You recently announced a partnership with athenahealth. Can you describe the nature of your relationship with them?

Kris Kiler: We recently developed an integration with athenahealth, inc. which is one of the larger cloud-based electronic health record (EHR) providers in the market with over 80,000 doctors on their system.

I believe they're the sixth largest EHR in the country. So, our Patient Promoter product is automated through the athenahealth EHR system. So, it's really a one-click service that automates the process of sending out all the reputation management emails on a daily basis. In addition, we also offer our marketing services and our monthly website design services on the athenahealth Marketplace, designed specifically for medical practices, to their medical practice clients.

About Kris Kiler

Kris Kiler is the president of Net One Click. Kris's passion for Internet marketing began in 1996 when he started using the Internet to market products and services. Since then he has worked with hundreds of companies to create and execute internet marketing plans that grow new customer channels, build upon current customer networks, and design brands that people love. An experienced entrepreneur, he understands making decisions with limited information in this complex world and approaches all clients with a strategic, results-focused approach.

Prior to founding Net One Click, Kris was president and chief executive officer of an organizational development company that focused on human performance training, book publishing, and Internet services. There he launched more than sixty products; including trade publishing books, adult learning materials, and psychological assessments; launched a line of human performance trainings to Fortune 500 companies, and developed and launched a cutting-edge client management and assessment delivery software-as-service (SAS) product. Kris has a passion for understanding what it takes to create great leaders. He is a certified Job and Career Transition Coach and an experienced instructional designer which provides him with skills in understanding how adults make decisions and learn new information. He was involved in the training and development field for over 15 years.

Kris works directly with all of Net One Click's clients to craft a plan that is unique to their business, industry, and budget. He is the author of *Ready, Aim, Capture!: The Secret to Successful Internet Marketing*, *Optimize Your Web Platform: A Small Business Guide to Internet Marketing Automation*, and coauthor of *Creating Multiple Streams of Income with Information Products: Turning Your Ideas Into Assets*.

WEBSITE
NetOneClick.com

EMAIL
kris@netoneclick.com

FACEBOOK
Facebook.com/NetOneClick

TWITTER
Twitter.com/netoneclick

Service, Value and Getting The Most from Your DJ Entertainment

A wedding is one of the most exciting events in a couple's life, but can also be the most stressful. Finding that many people are not knowledgeable or taking full advantage of everything that professional DJ Entertainers can offer, Teah-Jay Cartwright is on a mission to change that.

Teah-Jay and his team of DJ Entertainers at Soundman Music offer much more than music. Though music is the heart of the business, other outstanding levels of service are provided that most people are unaware of. They share common goals of their clients to create stand out events and unforgettable moments. Through the wide range of services offered, couples will soon realize that the value of a highly-trained DJ is beyond measure.

From coordination with other vendors to carrying a spare silver-plated cake knife in case it is forgotten on wedding day, Teah-Jay has thought of everything.

Teah-Jay will discuss the level of detail and organization a DJ can add to a wedding, allowing the bride, groom and guests to be free from all responsibility...except having fun and creating memories that will last a lifetime.

Conversation with Mr. Teah-Jay Cartwright W.P.I.C.C.

Tell us about Soundman Music and how you are helping your clients.

Teah-Jay Cartwright: It's the little details that often stress couples out the most...the things they didn't think about because they were overwhelmed or just didn't know it was something to consider. Sometimes in the rush of family and friends visiting for a wedding, people get distracted or things are forgotten and left behind. It's often something totally random and unexpected. These elements, although often minor in nature, can have a huge impact on a couples' satisfaction in their event, their self-confidence and how they think their guests will view them personally. They will often blame themselves or feel inadequate because something didn't go as planned or they didn't know to consider it in the first place.

I operated as a single DJ for nearly 10 years before adding on more staff and rebranding my business from TJ the DJ to Soundman Music. I have been fortunate enough to see both the multi-DJ company in operation and one on one interaction with clients. I have prepared my staff to look for the same things I do, to help them understand why and how important it is to be detail oriented and think beyond just being a DJ. Because a wedding is the most important and special day of couples' lives and thousands of dollars are spent on this event and similar ones, we make sure our clients are getting full value and beyond on these occasions. Music is important. It is the core of what we do, and there can be many layers surrounding that core.

Some examples of common hiccups are someone not being on time, heavy traffic, flat tires, photo location crowds, illness, items forgotten or simply not thought of. There is a lot for a couple to plan for and this is where professional quality vendors such as myself come in to help take care of some of that stress and planning. I take many things into consideration such as where to set up so as not to take away from the elegance of decorations, song selection, play/do not play lists, dedications, songs for special moments and engaging the entire crowd to make sure everyone is having a memorable time. I have decades of experience helping couples and have developed strategies with my staff to prevent every hiccup so that clients can feel confident when they choose Soundman Music.

On a day already charged with a lot of emotion and stress, little things left unchecked can completely alter the success of your special day. My goal is to work with you before your wedding day and network with your other vendors so that we are all on the same page, looking at everything from our own specialty viewpoints. Each of us will have a different take on the various events planned and what potential issues could arise. Ultimately, we all work together to achieve the results you want. This will give you more confidence, less stress, and the ability to enjoy every moment as the guests of honor with no worry of planning your event as it happens. The result of a happy, stress free couple will really shine through your photos, your guests will see and feel it, and that positive energy will transfer to the dance floor.

What are the advantages of creating an unforgettable, successful, and fun celebration for brides and planners of events, parties, and celebrations?

Teah-Jay Cartwright: Who doesn't love hearing other people boast about how good you are at something? When you plan an unforgettable event, it should be just that. Unforgettable for all the right reasons! You want to hear how others wish their wedding was like yours and how you were able to create an event that was fun and memorable for all.

It feels good. People remember for years and your photos will be shared and featured on their social media pages. This is part of the value of the services you receive when hiring Soundman Music. It's not just that your DJ played from 5pm to 1am (standard wedding hours in Canada) or that your photographer spent 10-12 hours with you starting before the ceremony to after the formal dances. There is a lot of work a professional will do BEFORE your event to be prepared AT your event so that AFTER everything is packed up and your vendors have left people are still complimenting you on their experience.

When I do my job as an entertainer, your guests will be smiling, sitting upright in their chairs, laughing and dancing. These are the photos you want your photographer to capture. If I am not doing my job people are not smiling, chairs are empty, people are slouched with their arms crossed and no one is dancing. Those are not the lasting memories you want to create.

Your photos will be a reminder of everything that happened. Does your photo album stay on the coffee table or does it get buried in the back of a closet?

How do you want to FEEL about your special day or event? How do you want to feel before, during and after? The entire experience should be unforgettable and stress free.

What do you feel are the biggest myths out there when it comes to creating an unforgettable, successful, and fun celebration?

Teah-Jay Cartwright: I would have to say the DIY culture. It's all about the money and not about what is truly important, not that money isn't. The fact is any event should involve the time needed to plan and prepare properly. It takes time to make sure there are no kinks and to iron out existing ones before they become an issue. It's not always an easy process. Depending on the type of event, the number of factors involved can range from a few to many…. how does everything interrelate? Where can your vendors cross wires? Are all your ideas possible?

Hiring professional, qualified vendors will help ensure you don't have issues, increase confidence, reduce stress and give you time to work on other aspects of your event more efficiently.

Budget is also a big deal. DIY is all about saving a buck, but are you? You can look for "affordable" and "reasonable" vendors, but if you have never planned an event before, as most people haven't, how do you know what is affordable or reasonable? What is fair value for the services offered? People fail to budget appropriately, even when taking a DIY approach. A wedding from engagement to honeymoon will likely cost as much as a small to medium sized car. In my area of Canada, the average wedding cost is between $22,000 and $29,000.

Many couples quote American blogs and sources for prices. They don't consider that costs are different in the Great White North where winter is often 6-8 months of the year. We have to pay for storage with heading year-round. All the gear we buy out of the U.S. has duty and exchange rates that we have to build into our prices. An average wedding day for a Canadian DJ can be 14-18 hours long, even if your reception is only seven hours long with a 90-minute ceremony (seating to guests exiting).

Couples will DIY their decor... they will buy what they need for exactly the number of centerpieces, for example. What if a mistake is made? Now you have to get more supplies. That's more time driving or ordering and more money spent. Or DIY flowers...buying what is needed and then finding out what you wanted isn't as easy as it looks in the Pinterest picture, you end up wasting flowers, or don't store them properly and they are wilted at the altar. You decide to DIY your music. You get all your songs on an iPod, you rent a speaker that sounds powerful and you ask a family member to switch the songs for you. Only to find out the speaker sounds tinny or distorted because you don't really understand how the wattage works, the iPod ends up playing six slow songs in a row, a vulgar song offends your guests, or the family member you asked to look after it is partying too much to handle their DJ responsibilities appropriately.

Did you really save money? Time? Stress? What else could you have been doing while your professional vendors did those things for you? What are your guests going to remember?

Couples will try to plan fast, think it's easy, and believe services should be cheaper than quoted. Sadly, there is someone out there that will take their money and are often not qualified or professional. I created Soundman Music as a response to those types of services because I was getting an increase in calls from couples whose "DJ" took their money and was never to be seen or heard from again, or cancelled weeks or days before their wedding.

It starts in the planning and budgeting. A great wedding will take up to a year to plan...sometimes longer if you really want to make it special. The more time you have, the more you can budget for and it will feel much easier. If you try to plan something in six months or less, you will have a shoestring budget, too much going on to think straight, and mistakes will be made. Someone forgets to ask the Emcee to Emcee, hotels don't get booked, someone forgets to make arrangements to pick up the suits or flowers, hasn't considered how to get the chairs from the ceremony to the hall, or forgets to unlock the hall so the DJ, decorator and caterers can't get in to set up. Unfortunately, these scenarios can and do happen.

What are some common misconceptions around the DJ Entertainment industry?

Teah-Jay Cartwright: The assumption that anyone can be a DJ. Oftentimes, people think all you need is an iPod and a random family member to talk on the mic and be the center of attention while simultaneously partying all night. A DJ costs too much and really, what do they do?

There was a time when being the DJ was respected. The gear cost a lot more than it does today. It was a lot more cumbersome to move and set up and it wasn't as easy to operate. For these reasons, people falsely believe it is easier to do.

I have been a Professional DJ for over 20 years. If you do something long enough at a professional level, it is going to look easy to anyone watching you.

What are some of the most common fears about creating an unforgettable, successful, and fun celebration?

Teah-Jay Cartwright: Couples often don't know what to ask. They don't have confidence in their ideas and they worry too much about cost and not enough about value. They hire someone and expect them to read their minds, don't communicate effectively and don't take the time to research the companies they contact or the services they want. It is similar to being a kid in a toy store and not understanding the concept of money or where it comes from. This is how many get taken advantage of or hire a terrible vendor which is ultimately their biggest fear.

How can they get past these fears?

Teah-Jay Cartwright: Get over the fear of a personal conversation. Communication is the #1 solution. Ask other vendors you may have spoken with for who they recommend, problems they have seen at other events, and then ask how each DJ would manage that problem. Look at their social media and websites and ask for their references or reviews. When you contact your perspective DJ do they offer to meet with you? Do they answer all your questions and do they give you lots of information answering questions you never thought to ask? A great vendor will overwhelm you with information you never asked for about problems, planning and situations they help you take care of.

Personality plays a HUGE role when working with your DJ. Does your DJ get your vision? Do they get your quirks and can they take your ideas and expand on them in a way that suits you as a couple? Do you feel like they "get you" and do you feel they have the ability to best represent you as a host to your family and friends? Your vendors should help you feel more confident! Hire professional, experienced vendors who will work together and encourage you and your ideas and actively help make them possible. Once we all have a good sense of what you want, we should be networking together to help make it happen. A wedding is like a production. There is sound, lighting, set design, food service, costumes, makeup, hair and so on. A movie is not made without all departments working together to make it happen. A wedding should be no different.

What other perceived obstacles do you see that might be preventing brides and event planners from seeking the help of a DJ Entertainer?

Teah-Jay Cartwright: General lack of knowledge in regards to the responsibilities and tasks a DJ performs, which often leads people to believe a Professional DJ is overpriced. The value of the services offered is in the details of the service. When someone sends me a one line message "What's your price?", it is really hard to start engaging with that person effectively. It tells me they have not taken the time to do any research and are not going to be fully aware of the services I offer. I have to first begin to educate before I can sell my services. It adds unnecessary steps to our communication that are tedious and frustrating for both of us. They just want to hire a DJ and I want to help them make an informed choice.

What are some of the little-known pitfalls or common mistakes you see brides and planners of events, parties, and celebrations make on the road to creating an unforgettable, successful, and fun celebration?

Teah-Jay Cartwright: Failing to budget appropriately, both time and money, before and throughout the planning process. Many couples don't take the time after booking vendors to stay in touch and access their wealth of knowledge and experience. Higher priced vendors will often include more time allowance for the couples to work with them in personal meetings and contacts. They will offer more services that relate specifically to the type of event through games, lighting, additional sound etc. A five-minute phone call or text isn't personal or always thorough enough to convey an idea or problem and source a solution that is fitting to the client's specific questions or situation.

How can these pitfalls / mistakes be avoided?

Teah-Jay Cartwright: Take your time. The more time you have before an event, the longer you have to budget. When you meet the professional vendor that gives you the confidence that they are the one for you, you can afford them too.

When first meeting with your vendors, don't be afraid to grill them. It's an interview for a very important position and you should feel confident in their experience to do what you need and capability of doing more. Don't underestimate the value of communication. Never be afraid to ask to meet for coffee. Touch base to re-familiarize yourself with the vendor. You may have booked them months ago, forgotten what they look like and half the conversation from the booking meeting. Go over all the details again...likely your thoughts have changed or you have decided to add or remove certain aspects of your overall plan. Make sure they will be available when you need them for follow-up discussion, idea sessions and open to being creative to make your event happen the way you envision it.

You must also be open to their knowledge and experience. They have seen things, tried things and should understand some of the difficulties of putting certain ideas into effect. There isn't much I have not seen in my years as a professional. What might be an original idea to you could be something I have tried before and I can offer ideas on how to make it happen successfully. It can save you a lot of time and potentially money.

Can you share an example of how you have helped your clients overcome these obstacles and succeed in creating an unforgettable, successful, and fun celebration?

Teah-Jay Cartwright: Here is a sample of the level of detail I am thinking about when working with my clients. You will notice that the actual DJing part happens at the very end.

Cutting of the cake is a traditional element of almost every wedding. Some people use cupcakes today or skip it entirely, but it is a tradition that has meaning. It's a physical representation of your vows, to love and care for each other and provide for the needs of the other person. The cake is a symbol of your love and feeding a piece of it to each other is a beautiful representation of nourishing and caring. A lot of the traditions have these deeper meanings that many people don't know about. To most it's just a $500 - $2500 cake. But I wanted to put it into some context so that you understand how a professional DJ can add meaning to both the small and large details of your event.

Most people have the cake in a corner or off to the side because they don't understand the importance. Also, if your favorite aunt made the cake or you paid $1000 for the cake, it's kind of an insult to have it off to the side. The cake cutting is only a brief moment, but it also provides the potential for so many great photos.

First, I am a Professional Entertainer. Entertainment is not just the DJ. It's the experience you are giving your guests. The look, the feel, the sounds. The WOW effect. So, as I tell this story, think of the WOW effect I am trying to help you create as part of my service. This is part of my price but not something I can easily list on a website:

You have instructed me on when you would like to cut the cake. That time is approaching. Rather than just blindly announcing that the cake cutting is in 5 minutes, I consider the following first:

Where is the cake table? I need to be able to direct your guests to it so they can take photos of you cutting it. I always recommend placing the cake table about 6-8 feet in front of the head table centered on the dance floor. The dance floor is often empty and it's the perfect space to showcase your cake. Your head table and backdrop are a perfect frame for the cake before your grand entrance and your guests can marvel at its creation. Often, I will add a light under the table so that it glows in one of your colours or is eye catching.

What's on the cake table? Is the cake on the table? Perhaps the cake is a tall tier or there are lots of kids around and you don't want finger holes poked in the icing. You can't announce the cake cutting without a cake. If it is not there, I will go to the kitchen and ask them to bring it out or talk with the banquet staff. I will also look to see what kind of decorations are on the table to help frame the cake. Are there flowers? Is the cake knife set there?

Is the photographer ready? I will then find the photographer. They are usually getting photos of guests and family members. I let them know it is time for the cake cutting as they are often busy and may need a minute or two to set up remote flashes and choose their angles.

Are YOU ready? I will look for the couple, tracking down the bride first in most cases. I will ask if you are ready before I give the 5-minute warning announcement. I will ask if you would like to have your bouquet added to the table to help frame the cake if the table is otherwise plain. I will ask where your cake knives are if not at the table and I will find the groom if needed as he is usually outside talking and drinking with his buddies. Perhaps someone needs a bathroom break first.

Often enough, at least two times a year, the cake knives are forgotten. Usually someone leaves them at home on a counter or they are lost in a vehicle. Couples then resort to the big yellow handled roast carving knife. Imagine... we have framed your cake with your elegantly decorated head table and backdrop, you picked a song that you feel reflects the fun part of your relationship, we have added a bouquet or two around the base of the cake adding to the overall look of beauty, and you have a 20-inch serrated yellow handled mini machete to carve your cake with... it will stand out and take away from everything else, especially your photos.

I bring my own set of silver-handled cake knives just in case.

But wait... there's more. You now have everything you need and it looks wonderful. I announce the cake cutting to family and friends, and encourage them to gather around and place bets on who will wear the most icing.

Before everyone walks away, there is another great opportunity to get even more photos and have a little fun! We are on the dance floor and there is a lot of room around the cake. I will have you step around the cake facing the head table, backs to the guests. I will call up all the guests to gather on the dance floor. The photographer stands behind the head table (I usually bring a step ladder), and we get some group shots of everyone in fun poses...happy cheering, bored on the phone, scared, everyone jumping with hands in the air, etc.

In this example, I have worked with your caterer/ venue staff, photographer and in some cases, the bakery that provided the cake. We have taken what is typically a 60 second cake cutting in a corner with a plain wall backdrop and made it into something really fun. We allowed all your guests to be involved and took advantage of the wonderful photo opportunities as a result.

I played one song during all of this and made a couple announcements. A DJ isn't about just music (at least I'm not). I'm about helping you create the memorable moments your photographer will capture and creating entertainment your guests will remember.

How many problems did I potentially solve by taking the time to ensure everyone and everything was ready? The couple gets to sit back and savor every moment, without worrying about a thing. Your professional vendors just made it happen with fantastic results!

What inspired you to become a DJ Entertainer?

Teah-Jay Cartwright: I wanted to become a radio DJ. As early as seventh grade, I was fascinated by this personality I could hear coming out of the radio. That person sounded like they were always having fun and had a following of people who "hung out" with them and enjoyed their show. I really enjoyed listening to music and making my own mix tapes off the radio.

For those who are reading this wondering what I am talking about...these were the days before computers. You would use a tape recorder or your radio would have a built-in cassette deck and you could record from the speaker or directly from the radio. You had to time it just right from when the radio guy stopped talking to record the song and then stop it when they started talking again. It was a process.

I was bullied in school a lot for my looks. I was born with a hair-lip and cleft palate. Although I didn't sound or talk funny, I still had the odd scar under my nose to my lip and my nose was a little lopsided because of it. I grew up being very self-conscious about my looks, but I loved to talk and socialize.

Radio just felt like the natural solution. No one would know what I looked like and I could still be that happy voice that people were drawn to. I didn't know how to get into radio and when I finished high school I started researching. While I was saving up for "radio school", I answered an ad to become a DJ. It sounded like fun. It was similar to radio, but I didn't need to pay to go to school for it. The company was going to pay me.

I did eventually go to "radio school" but by then radio had gone from fun and free to corporate and commercial and I didn't enjoy it at all, always having to be scripted to promote and advertise. It was much different from what I enjoyed listening to as I was growing up.

I was still in the dark part of the room, not really seen, and I could watch the effect I was having on people. They were having fun, laughing...and it had nothing to do with my looks. I still got comments like "Not bad for a hair-lip". Although those comments hurt, they just drove me to be better. I wanted to prove that my looks didn't impact my ability to entertain.

Back then DJing was a lot simpler. I started with cassette tapes. I didn't have a lot of time to do extra stuff between songs as I was listening to songs on fast forward to find the next song I wanted to play. Today, thanks to technology, I have more time between songs, but it's harder to entertain people. That same technology is in everyone's hands and they are distracted by social media and gaming apps. People are less social and despite being in a room full of friends and family, they sit at tables and stare into their mobile devices.

Can you share a lesson you learned early on, that still impacts how you do business today?

Teah-Jay Cartwright: I was a terrible DJ when I started. I was not a natural. I was decent, but I look at what I have learned and I feel like I should find some of those old clients from 20+ years ago and give them their money back. Mind you, weddings were $500 for a DJ then. Now $2000 is more the average for a professional.

I was still self-conscious. I wouldn't put myself into the spotlight. I noticed the little things that people missed or that took away from the wedding but I was not truly engaging. I had to really work on my self-confidence. Finally, one night it clicked. The couple was awesome, friendly and gracious. Their families were very kind people and I took to the dance floor to teach people a few line dances I had learned. The Macarena and Cotton Eyed Joe. I felt very embarrassed and self-conscious and I tried not to let it show. Before long, I had everyone up doing the steps with me and thanking me. I got my very first tip at the end of the night and the boss got a great thank you card (this is before e-mail). It showed me that if I stopped worrying so much about what bad could happen, I would have a lot more good in my life.

What's the most important question brides and planners of events, parties, and celebrations should ask themselves as they consider creating an unforgettable, successful, and fun celebration?

Teah-Jay Cartwright: What memories do you want to create? What do you want people to remember most about your special day? What moments do you really want to have stand out in people's minds?

How delicious the food was? How the hall looked? How people danced and celebrated all night? People won't remember all the details so pick out what you think is going to set your celebration apart. They may not remember it was your wedding, but they will remember what stood out about it and you can take joy in reminding them whose wedding it was and have a great time reliving all of those special moments.

What's the most important thing brides and planners of events, parties, and celebrations should consider when evaluating a DJ Entertainer?

Teah-Jay Cartwright: I hope I have demonstrated the importance of meeting in person with your DJ before booking. Look for someone who isn't "just a DJ" that "only plays music". You want someone knowledgeable, experienced, and open to your ideas. They should possess the creativity to make suggestions that accentuate your ideas or offer alternatives if needed. You want your DJ, and all vendors, to be detail oriented. They should understand what the roles of your other vendors are and be willing to work with them as your point person.

You need to feel you can trust them and have confidence they can do what they say they can. We are all on the same team (your team), and should be helping you every step of the way. Additionally, keep in mind that quality, professional vendors don't come cheap. You get more than you pay for and there is always great value in the price. Make the effort to budget accordingly.

How can someone find out more about Teah-Jay Cartwright and Soundman Music and how you can help?

Teah-Jay Cartwright: Google me. My name is very unique and I am pretty easy to find on Facebook. I am based in Red Deer, Alberta Canada and I serve all three

Western Provinces with my company, Soundman Music. Soundman Music is a multi-op DJ service with trained, experienced DJ entertainers who can take your event to the next level. You can contact us on social media, email and by text or phone.

Our website is www.soundmanmusic.com. We keep it pretty simple and easy to use and you can contact me directly through our site. Even if you are not in my service area, I try to help people as much as I can. I believe everyone should have the best possible wedding they can achieve.

I focus everyday on being positive and feeling grateful for where I am, and thankful for all the people who helped get me here. Thank you for taking the time to read my thoughts. It is my hope that I will help you to create a more memorable event.

About Mr. Teah-Jay Cartwright
W.P.I.C.C.

Teah-Jay Cartwright started his Mobile DJ career in June 1996 at the age of 19. He graduated from Western Academy Broadcasting College in 2006 and went on to become a Certified Wedding Planner through the Wedding Planner Institute of Canada in 2011.

Teah-Jay began working for a Company Called A.C.M. (American Classic Music) which was bought out by Soundman Music's original owner who retired from the business himself and closed the company in 2006. Teah-Jay made the decision to better himself and further his training in a college Radio Broadcasting program. He started his own DJ company in 2008 called "TJ the DJ" and rebranded in 2019 to Soundman Music as a multi-op DJ company. Soundman had an excellent name and reputation that people still remember today.

In addition to his musical interests, Teah-Jay decided to run for politics in 2019 as a member of the Legislative Assembly of Alberta, which is a provincial government position. He is currently waiting for the results and is hopeful for a win.

Teah-Jay resides and works out of Red Deer, Alberta Canada. He provides services to both neighbouring provinces with a growing staff of professionally trained Music Entertainers.

WEBSITE
SoundManMusic.com

EMAIL
info@soundmanmusic.com

LinkedIn
Teah-Jay Cartwright

INSTAGRAM
SoundmanMusic

PHONE
403-348-1224

www.ingramcontent.com/pod-product-compliance
Lightning Source LLC
Chambersburg PA
CBHW071527200326
41519CB00019B/6104